VANISHING HABITATS

First published in Canada in 2009 by
Scholastic Canada Ltd.
175 Hillmount Road
Markham, Ontario
L6C 1Z7

10 9 8 7 6 5 4 3 2 1

Library and Archives Canada Cataloguing
    in Publication
Bateman, Robert, 1930-
    Vanishing habitats / Robert Bateman.
ISBN 978-0-545-98621-2
    1. Bateman, Robert, 1930- --Juvenile literature.
2. Endangered species in art--Juvenile literature.
3. Animals in art--Juvenile literature. 4. Wildlife
conservation--Juvenile literature. 5. Habitat
conservation--Juvenile literature.
I. Title.

ND249.B3175A4 2009 j759.11 C2009-901808-X

Printed in China

VANISHING HABITATS

Robert Bateman

with Nancy Kovacs

A SCHOLASTIC / MADISON PRESS BOOK

It really isn't news that the natural world
is shrinking. We constantly hear about
global warming, the cutting down of
rainforests, and the disappearance of fields
and forests to make way for growing cities.
When these natural areas disappear, wild plants and animals
lose their habitats. This is the bad news. The good news is
that some people are working to protect these habitats and
the animals and plants that live in them.

   If we want to save our wildlife, we need to know about
where they live. In this book I will show you some of the
places that may vanish if we do not save them. I hope that
it will start you on your own journey to learn what you can
do to help protect the world's natural treasures.

Robert Bateman

Introduction

When I was a child in Toronto, I could step out my back door and climb down to a ravine rich in natural beauty. This ravine had been carved out by an ancient river that dried up long ago, leaving behind a world completely different from the city outside my front door. Here was a forest filled with plants and creatures I had never imagined, a fascinating and constantly changing world.

I spent as much of my free time in the ravine as I could, watching and learning. In spring, I marveled at the colorful warblers migrating north. In spring and summer, I studied the wildflowers. In autumn, as leaves turned to red and orange and yellow, I saw songbirds flying back to their southern homes. And in winter, amid the silent snow, I observed deer and foxes and the hardy birds that stayed in spite of the cold.

I did not know then how small my forest was compared to the vast forest that had once been there. And when I visit Toronto today, I see how much more has been lost since I was a child. There are still ravines and parks, but there are far more buildings and roads. Birds still migrate through the ravines, but in smaller numbers. Compared to the city of my childhood, so much has vanished.

When natural habitats are destroyed, so much is lost. Birds and animals depend on them for food, shelter, and nesting places. Plants and trees provide food for insects, birds, and animals. The insects and animals are food for other animals and birds. All of this wildlife provides nutrients that help trees and plants to grow. Water habitats are also part of this cycle. Plants and animals alike depend on the clean water for survival.

This book will describe many types of natural habitat in our world, like grasslands, deserts, lakes, rivers, oceans, and forests of all kinds. It will tell you why many of them are vanishing and what some people are doing to try to help. I hope that it will inspire you to learn more about nature, both in your neighborhood and around the world.

What is a Habitat?

This stream bank may seem only a tangle of leaves, vines, and branches, but within that tangle are insects, worms, salamanders, small mammals, and birds. You can almost see the leaves rustling as the creatures scurry about their business. All those plants and animals depend on each other to survive, and yet the bank does not stay the same. For many years I passed

it during walks from my home in southern Ontario, noticing how it changed from season to season. But the changes were not just because of the seasons—ten years after I painted the bank, it was entirely different. A tree had crashed into the middle of the tangle, the stream's edge was altered, and the species that lived there had changed. It was still a vibrant habitat, but not the one I had originally painted.

A habitat is a place where animals and plants can live and find enough food to survive. It is the soil, the rocks, the water, the wildlife, the plants, the trees, and the climate in a particular place. Everything works together. In its proper habitat, a plant gets sunlight, water, and nutrition. An animal's habitat provides food and water, protection from predators, nesting material, and a place to raise and protect its young.

A habitat can be large or small. A whole forest is the habitat for some species, but within it are many smaller habitats. Insects live under a tree's bark. Some animals live on the forest floor, while others stay high in the trees. A newly hatched bird must stay in its nest, but once able to fly it will make its way in the larger world outside. A farmer's field is home to

Mountain goats live in the high mountains of North America. Sure-footed and agile, these herbivores eat the moss, lichen, grasses, and woody plants that grow at these heights.

mice and other small mammals. Some fish live their lives among the weeds in a lake. Some whales migrate great distances through the ocean each year. Along a lakeshore or stream bank are crayfish and water insects and larvae. Even a dog's fur can be a habitat—for fleas!

Many birds and animals migrate with the seasons, while others move only when food runs short. Salamanders are born in the water, but move to dry land when they are grown and never go into the water again.

Some creatures can live in a variety of habitats. Mice flourish in fields and woods and even in people's houses. Other animals have very specific needs that are met only by one particular habitat. For example, panda Bears must live where bamboo grows because it is their main source of food. These animals are the most affected when their habitats start to disappear, because they cannot find food elsewhere.

Habitats are only part of the picture, though. We use the word "habitat" to refer to a place where a particular species lives. An "ecosystem," on the other hand, is a place where many species exist together. One animal may be food for another. Plants and trees provide food and shelter for a variety of creatures. Even the climate plays its part. It is the interaction of all of these factors—plants, trees, animals, insects, birds, water, terrain, and climate—that make up an ecosystem. It is important to understand that threats to a single habitat have an impact far beyond a few species.

Forests

Forests grow throughout the world, except near the poles. They can be made up of all deciduous (or broadleaf) trees, all coniferous (or evergreen) trees, or both. Deciduous trees have leaves that fall off when the tree is dormant. Coniferous trees have needle-like leaves that are shed and renewed all year round. They carry their seeds in resin-filled cones that protect them from weather and intruders.

Many species inhabit forests, from the Japanese macaque that lives in both cold and warm forests to the many deer that feed on the leaves in temperate forests. Birds nest in tree holes or on branches. Insects live under the bark or in the leaves on the forest floor.

Once, gray wolves roamed forests all over the world. They are now all but extinct everywhere except for North America. The reasons are many. They were often hunted for their skins and to protect farmers' livestock. Sometimes the animals they preyed on were hunted by people as well, leaving them too little to eat. And sometimes the forests where they lived were completely or partially cut down.

Fragmentation is the biggest problem facing our forests today. Fragmentation happens when forests are cut into pieces to make room for towns, cities, and farms to grow our food. This affects the wildlife in many ways. First, smaller forests have fewer species than larger forests, because there is less food and shelter to go around. Second, some species thrive only in the deepest parts of a forest. These species are more vulnerable to threats in a smaller forest. Third, many migratory birds will follow only a forested route. If there is no uninterrupted forest, they cannot reach their summer nesting areas.

There are some solutions. We can encourage the growth of new forest, and protect the forest that exists. We can also leave strips of trees between forested areas to provide a continuous migration route.

Japanese macaques, also called snow monkeys, are found everywhere in Japan, in colder regions than any other monkey in the world. They are endangered because of habitat loss, which includes not only their home, but the loss of the fruit and seeds they eat.

The white-tailed deer lives in deciduous forests from Canada to South America. It has also been introduced to New Zealand and a few countries in Europe.

FACTS

* *

* Some types of deciduous trees
  are maples, elms, oaks, birches,
  hickory, and walnut.

* Some types of coniferous trees
  are firs, pines, spruce, cedar,
  and hemlock.

* The tallest species of tree is
  the "coast" Redwood.

* Tasmania, off the coast of
  Australia, has the second tallest
  species, the Australian
  mountain-ash.

Boreal Forests

In the high Arctic, only a few shrubs and plants live. Further south are more and more trees, until finally we reach the dense boreal forest. A ring of brilliant green encircling our earth, boreal forests are great expanses of coniferous trees—spruce, pines, and firs—and a few deciduous trees, like birches, that can withstand the cold climate.

Many animals make their homes in boreal forests. Bears, caribou, wolves, foxes, and lynx are just a few. Some, like bears, hibernate in the winter. Others grow thick fur. Very few birds stay all winter, but around 300 species nest there each summer, including many small songbirds that migrate from tropical regions.

The boreal forest may seem permanent, but there are threats to it and its inhabitants. Logging destroys hundreds of thousands of acres each year, endangering species like gray wolves, lynx, and woodland caribou. Songbirds lose their nesting sites and are also harmed by pesticides used by loggers to control insects like the spruce budworm.

Global warming affects the boreal wildlife. As temperatures increase, the climate of these vast ecosystems is changing. These changing weather conditions will result in more forest fires and insect outbreaks, increasing the challenges to all the forest's wildlife.

Many of the inhabitants of the boreal forests need the vast expanse of trees in order to thrive. The Siberian tiger lives in the cold northern forests of eastern Russia. Like all tigers it is endangered. Intensive logging has destroyed or fragmented its forest habitat. There are fewer wild boar and deer—the tiger's favorite food—because of habitat loss. Finally, humans hunt the tiger for its fur and body parts. There are fewer than 400 Siberian tigers left. They are protected, but their status must be watched if they are to survive.

Gray wolves, or timber wolves, are the largest of all wild dog-like animals. Their paws have webbing that helps them walk on snow. This helps them especially in the snows of the boreal forest.

There are only a few hundred Siberian tigers left in the world. The largest of all wild cats, it is a victim of habitat loss. It has also traditionally been killed for its body parts, used in ancient Chinese medicines. This practice is now illegal, but it still goes on.

FACTS

···

✳ The temperature in boreal forests is very cold, averaging around 30° F (0° C). It can get down to -65° F (-50° C) in the winter!

✳ Boreal forests get about 30 inches (75 cm) of rain a year.

✳ Another name for the northern parts of the boreal forest is taiga.

✳ The deepest parts of a boreal forest are so dense that very little sunlight gets through and no small trees or shrubs grow there.

✳ Bogs are common in boreal forests, where they are called muskeg.

Temperate Forests

Between the boreal forest and the tropical rainforests, the climate is temperate. Hot in the summer and cold in winter, temperate areas receive moderate amounts of rainfall. Temperate forests can be deciduous, coniferous, or a combination of both, and they are found in North and South America, Europe, and Asia.

Temperate forests provide habitats for hundreds of bird and animal species. Some, like deer, coyotes, and many birds of prey, stay along the forest edges, moving in and out of the forest. Some prefer the deepest parts of the forest, where their nests are safer.

For centuries, temperate forests have been cut down for lumber, agriculture, and development. Many paper products, glossy magazines, and catalogues are still made from newly cut wood instead of recycled paper. Less forest means more competition for food and nesting space. It also leaves the door open to predators of all kinds.

One danger to a bird's nest is the brown-headed cowbird of North America. This parasite bird lays its eggs in the nests of other birds. The eggs hatch earlier than those of the host bird, and the young cowbirds are given preferential treatment. Often the host birds' young do not survive. The cowbird is a bird of open field, so when the forests were denser and more expansive, its impact was not great. Now, though, the forests have been so fragmented that the nests of many more birds are available for the cowbird's eggs, including those of the beautiful scarlet tanager and the wood thrush, whose hauntingly beautiful song echoes through the forest.

Like many colorful songbirds, scarlet tanagers molt their brilliant feathers after breeding and are quite drab-looking in their tropical winter homes.

The only warbler with a bright orange throat, the Blackburnian warbler nests in coniferous and mixed forests.

Tropical Rainforests

Tropical rainforests grow near the equator. Their tall trees reach into the sky and a canopy of leaves keeps the sun's rays from the forest floor. Specially adapted plants called epiphytes—orchids, mosses, and ferns—cling by their roots to tree branches, drawing moisture and nutrients from the air. Hot and humid, the tropical rainforest is full of constant activity.

Rainforests produce about 40 percent of the world's oxygen. They provide a home for over half of all living species in the world. Around 25 percent of modern medicines are made from tropical plants, and foods like chocolate, coffee, mangoes, and bananas all come from the rainforest. Rainforests are being cut down at an alarming rate. The trees are used for furniture, buildings, paper, and charcoal. The land is cleared for crops and as grazing land for farm animals. This is being done so fast that there could be no rainforest left in as little as 40 years. Hundreds of animals are being affected. In Africa, the forest home of the mountain gorilla is being destroyed for mining, development and farming; forest fragmentation restricts the habitat of the golden lion tamarin of Brazil; and the burning of the forest to make way for pasture is seriously affecting the ring-tailed lemur in Madagascar.

The jaguar prefers to hunt in dense forest where it is not easily seen by its prey. As the rainforest has become more fragmented, the jaguar has less area in which to live. It will take livestock from farms if necessary, and is often shot.

People are realizing that there is natural wealth in the rainforest. Medicines and foods can be harvested without cutting down the trees, while profits for farmers and governments will actually be greater. There is much still to be learned and done, but there is some hope that what remains of the rainforest can be saved.

The jaguar was a symbol of strength, courage and power for many ancient South and Central American cultures. The jaguar lives on up to eighty different prey animals—including turtles and alligators!

Mountain gorillas are shy and gentle unless provoked. They spend more time on the ground than other primates. There are only around 700 mountain gorillas left, and their numbers are decreasing due to loss of habitat, hunting, and disease.

FACTS

∗ The rainforests of Indonesia and Papua New Guinea may be completely gone in 20 years at the present pace of destruction.

∗ Tropical rainforests get at least 69 inches (175 cm) of rain each year. The temperature does not go below 64°F (18° C).

∗ The Amazon rainforest, the largest in the world, will be more than half destroyed in 20 years.

∗ Once very extensive, tropical rainforests now cover less than 6 percent of the earth's surface.

∗ More than half of all living species spend all or part of their lives in the rainforest.

FACTS

* Old growth forests are usually defined as being at least 150–200 years old, but some have trees that are thousands of years old.

* Russia has 20 percent of the remaining old growth forests left in the world.

* A bristlecone pine tree in California named Methuselah is the oldest tree on earth. It is around 5,000 years old!

* A Norway spruce in Sweden has a root system 10,000 years old, but the tree growing from the roots is only about 600 years old. Over the centuries the tree has died back many times, and new shoots have sprouted from the roots, growing into a new tree.

Old Growth Forests

The digestive system of pandas is like that of their carnivorous bear relatives, but unlike other bears, pandas live on a diet of plants.

The young spotted owl is entirely white at birth. As it matures, it turns brown and gains the spots that give the species its names.

Old Growth forests are the granddaddies of the earth's forests. Whether tropical or temperate, deciduous, coniferous, or mixed, these forests have survived untouched for hundreds or thousands of years. They are home to many species of plants and animals that prefer to be left undisturbed.

Several years ago, I moved with my family to the west coast of Canada. Our home is near the South Carmanah forest, one of the few old growth forests left in the world. It is home to the Carmanah giant—a Sitka spruce that measures 100 yards (95 meters) high! Several years ago, I was one of a group of artists invited to visit and paint the forest. Even as we painted, we could hear chainsaws, and nearby was a section of forest that had recently been cut down. The contrast between the beauty of the intact forest and the devastation of the logged section became the subject of my painting. Perhaps we did help—much of the Carmanah Valley is now protected by law.

The northern spotted owl inhabits old growth forests in North America. It nests in holes in the old trees and stays in the same area for life. It cannot recover if its habitat disappears. Spotted owls were in serious decline in the northwestern U.S. until a 1994 law limited logging in its old growth habitats. The owls did recover somewhat, but there is constant pressure to increase logging in the area.

Pandas live in old growth forests in China. When I visited a nature preserve in Sichuan Province, I felt right at home, as the trees were the same as those that grow in the Pacific Northwest—pine, fir, hemlock, larch, and birch. The bamboo plants in these forests are the food that pandas eat the most. In fact, pandas eat two different types of bamboo. When one variety dies off after flowering, the panda will seek out the other type. Clearing and fragmentation of their forests, and loss of access to their food, means that this fascinating animal is endangered.

FACTS

∗ There are both tall-grass and short-grass prairies in North America. Tall-grass prairies get a lot of rain, while short-grass prairies are drier and have hot summers and cold winters.

∗ Millions of bison roamed the prairies before being hunted almost to extinction.

∗ Steppes are cold grasslands with very poor soil. They are found in the U.S. and parts of Asia and eastern Europe.

∗ Herd animals like the pronghorn antelope are often trapped by the fences that separate fields in the Prairies, making their survival difficult.

Grassland: Prairies

The grizzly bear once roamed a huge territory that extended much further south than it does today. Now it is found only in western Canada and the north-western U.S.

Imagine an area without trees or shrubs, only mile after mile of grasses and wildflowers waving in the breeze. This habitat, called grassland, occurs on every continent in the world except Antarctica. While grassland usually has long spells of dry weather, it still gets more rain than a desert.

Long ago, much of central North America was a rich grassland, or prairie, with a thriving diversity of wildlife. The prairie had long periods of drought, but its plants were well adapted to survive. Millions of bison roamed its great expanse, together with swift foxes, grizzly bears, and prairie dogs.

Today, very few areas of natural prairie remain. Early settlers plowed the fields for farming, destroying the native plants, and introduced new crops like wheat and corn. The wonderful diversity of the grassland was gone, with some species probably lost forever. Fortunately, some people collected seeds from as many prairie plants as they could. They are working to reintroduce native plants into areas set aside for this purpose. In time, they hope to restore some of the beauty of the prairies.

The burrowing owl is a prairie bird. This little predator digs burrows in the ground for its nest. Conservationists have been concerned about its survival for a long time, because its habits and the farmers' seasons do not always match up. If farmers plow their fields early in the season, they destroy the owls' nests and eggs. Some farmers now wait for the eggs to hatch before they plow the ground, but if global warming provides an earlier planting season for farmers, things could once again worsen for the little owl.

The swift fox needs great expanses of prairie grassland to thrive. It was endangered in the 1930s when people wanted to control animals like wolves and coyotes that preyed on farm animals.

23

FACTS

* Savannas are transitional areas between forest and desert. Their climate is not as wet as a forest nor as dry as a desert, but they link the two.

* Savannas have two seasons, a very wet summer and a long, dry winter.

* The African savanna has trees like the acacia and the baobab.

* The South American savannas are known as pampas.

Grassland: The African Savanna

The so-called "King of the Jungle" doesn't live in the jungle at all. The African lion lives mostly on the savanna. The lion's numbers have greatly decreased in the last twenty years, due to habitat loss and killing by humans to protect livestock.

Dik-diks are small antelopes that prefer open grassland where they can see predators approaching.

Africa has an incredible variety of habitats, from rainforest to desert, but did you know that half of Africa's land is savanna? Savannas are usually found in warmer climates, like Australia and South America. The African savanna is rolling grassland dotted with a few woody shrubs and trees.

Hoofed mammals like zebras, wildebeest, antelopes, giraffes, and rhinoceros range the savanna in search of fresh water and food. Leopards, cheetahs, and lions follow the herds, taking advantage of weak or straggling members. Giant elephants are often nearby, using their strong trunks to pull up tough grasses to eat.

Plants in the savanna have clever ways to survive both the long dry seasons and the constant grazing of plant-eating animals. Many grow long taproots that seek out underground water sources. Others store water in bulbs. Most plants would die if their tops were constantly eaten off, but some savanna plants grow from the bottom instead of the top.

The African wild dog is endangered because the savanna has been fragmented or partially destroyed. These small dogs need lots of territory to stalk and bring down their prey. With less territory, they must compete with larger predators. Development is also a problem for them, as more contact with humans and their animals spreads disease to the wild dogs. To add to their difficulties, they are often killed by humans.

Many African species are endangered, but there is a good news story in Africa as well. Many of its governments have set aside lands for wildlife parks that preserve great expanses of land for these animals, keeping them safe from development and hunting.

Deserts: Hot and Cold

What is a desert? Is it a hot, dry place, or is it cold and windswept? Does it have huge sand dunes, or does it have miles of smooth white ice? Does it have almost no plants and animals, or is it a habitat for specially adapted plants and animals?

The answer is that a desert can be either hot or cold. Its surface can be sand, clay, pebbles—even ice. It may provide a home for many plants and animals suited to its special conditions—or next to none.

What do deserts have in common? They are found on every continent on earth, and they are always dry. They experience extreme temperatures, and they can be important habitats for many fascinating plants and animals.

For example, the saguaro cactus, a true giant of the cactus family, grows only in the hot Sonoran Desert of North America. Like all cacti, it stores water to survive the dry months, replenishing itself during the Sonoran's two rainy periods. Its spine-shaped leaves protect it from unwanted intruders. As it ages, cracks form in its trunk. Cactus wrens build nests in the cracks and insects take up residence; hawks perch on the saguaro to scan for prey, somehow avoiding injury from the sharp spines.

Unfortunately, human beings are changing the Sonoran Desert. They are introducing new plant species and crops that force out native grasses. Water is piped in to irrigate the new plants, making areas of the desert wetter and more fertile. This threatens the existence of desert species like the saguaro and other cacti, which rot when given too much water. The desert wildlife, too, is unable to adjust to these new conditions.

The Sahara Desert in northern Africa is another extremely hot and dry desert. Much of it can support some wildlife, but it has vast areas of sand seas and dunes, where fierce windstorms blow up walls of swirling sand. Only its oases, watered by underground springs, are able to sustain life.

The Sahara's nutrient-rich sands are important for a surprising reason. Although it is hard to believe, the fierce Sahara winds blow sand not only

Harris's hawks hunt in groups, which is unusual for birds of prey. Here they are perched on an old saguaro cactus. They also nest in cavities in these old cacti.

26

FACTS

* The largest deserts in the world are in the Arctic and Antarctica.

* Europe has only one true desert, the Tabernas Desert in Andalusia, Spain.

* Deserts cover about 14 percent of the earth's land.

* The desert of Antarctica is more than 5 million square miles (more than 13 million square km).

* The Arctic fox lives in the Arctic all year round and eats lemmings and other small animals, eggs, fish, and carrion (the leftovers of another animal's kill).

across the land, but right over the Atlantic Ocean! At the end of this journey, the sand falls in the Amazonian rainforests, where it becomes part of the soil and adds much-needed nutrients to the rainforest. Scientists fear that climate change will result in more rain falling in the Sahara. Wet sand cannot be blown such great distances, and the rainforests will lose this essential source of nutrients.

The Arctic tundra, at the North Pole, has the milder climate of the two polar deserts. Low plants and shrubs dot the landscape and many birds and animals call the Arctic home, at least part of the year. In springtime, when some of the ice melts, the tundra is an explosion of beautiful flowers and multi-colored lichen, and thousands of birds return from warmer climates to nest.

Ostriches are able to retain enough water to last them several days, a trait that serves them well in the dry desert. They have a powerful kick that can severely injure or kill any animal that corners them.

Gentoo penguins swim faster underwater than any other penguin. Overfishing of their prey fish, pollution, and disturbance of their breeding areas may be causing their numbers to go down.

Antarctica, at the South Pole, is a huge layer of rock covered by ice. Only cold-weather plants like mosses and lichens grow here. Its animal life spends much of its time in the water, usually migrating to warmer climates during the harsh winter. Its most famous inhabitants are its penguins, flightless birds that thrive in the frigid conditions.

FACTS

* *

* Amphibians (like frogs, toads, salamanders, and newts) have very sensitive skin and react quickly to changes in their environment.

* About one third of all amphibian species are threatened with extinction because of global warming, pollution, and habitat loss.

Wetlands

The beaver dam has flooded the river, creating shallow wetlands—the right habitat for the aquatic plants that moose like to eat.

The hooded crane breeds in bogs and winters in marshes, rice paddies, and other wetlands. Cranes are beautiful, elegant birds that have been admired for centuries, and yet their habitats are under constant threat from development and dams.

People used to believe that wetlands were unpleasant, dirty places with no value. They decided it was best to drain them for farms, homes, and shopping malls. It is known now that wetlands are valuable habitats. They support a great variety of plant and animal life. They filter out pollution from the water and pass nutrients on to the surrounding environment. They can store excess water after severe rainstorms, protecting surrounding areas from floods. And they store massive amounts of carbon—when a wetland is destroyed it releases the gas into the air, contributing to global warming!

In spite of what has been learned, many people still do not value wetlands, so they are still at risk. Development is probably the biggest concern, but there are other problems as well. Spraying for mosquitoes is one of the worst, and not just because the pesticide gets into the food chain. The bigger problem is that eliminating the mosquitoes takes away an important food source for dragonflies, bats, and birds, putting their survival at risk.

Wetlands are bodies of very shallow water that are usually connected to other bodies of water, like lakes or rivers. They are also found along ocean coastlines. Wetlands' water can be fresh, salty, or brackish (slightly salty) and either standing, which means it doesn't flow, or slowly flowing. There are wetlands everywhere, even in Antarctica during its short summer. The three best-known types are marshes, swamps, and bogs.

Throughout the world, wildlife has been threatened by the destruction of these vibrant habitats. We have learned much about the importance of the world's wetlands, but we must keep insisting that they be preserved.

Marshes

A marsh is a large, open, shallow wetland having plants like grasses, reeds, and water lilies. There are usually no trees, but sometimes shrubs grow along its shoreline. In the water, you will see insects, turtles, and fish. Marshes are most important as habitats for ducks, geese, and other waterfowl.

Swamps

A swamp is not all water. Small areas of land emerge, dotting the water. The plant life is quite different from that in a marsh. There are trees and shrubs along the shores that don't mind being waterlogged from time

The pintail is a dabbling duck, tipping its tail up and head down into the shallow marsh water to feed on underwater plants. Pintails are found in northern areas around the world.

The pitcher plant is a carnivorous plant. Its pitcher is a deep cavity full of liquid. Insects fall into the liquid and drown, and the plant gradually absorbs nutrients as the bodies decompose.

The red-eyed tree frog lives in the South American rainforest, laying its eggs in the temporary pools left after the rainforest's rainy periods.

to time. The life in swamps is very diverse. Animals like deer, opossums, and raccoons are common. Water birds, frogs, woodpeckers, snakes, turtles, alligators, and insects—all these and hundreds more species make swamps their home.

Bogs

Bogs are wetlands found only in cool temperate climates around the world. A bog is a shallow, very still body of water. Its soil and water have very little oxygen. You will recognize a bog because it has lots of moss growing in it. This moss and the other plant life decompose very slowly. Carnivorous plants, like the pitcher plant, thrive in bogs because they get their nutrition from insects, not the soil. Few animals live in bogs because there is very little open water. Some birds nest on the bog and a few animals venture out to steal the birds' eggs, but the buzzing of dragonflies and other insects is the sound you will hear most often.

Other Wetlands

Vernal pools are temporary shallow pools formed by spring rains and melted snow that dry up in summer. (Vernal means spring.) Vernal pools are crucial for the life cycle of certain amphibians, including many species of frogs and salamanders. The eggs of these animals are laid in vernal pools. The emerging tadpoles live in the pools until they have grown legs, lost their gills, and moved onto dry ground to live out their lives.

Lakes

Nothing is more magical than a lake early in the morning. The water is still and the air is clear, but the wildlife is active. Fish swim around underwater rocks and plants; ducks paddle on the surface; and dragonflies dart through the air. Above the surface, kingfishers dive after unsuspecting fish. Along the shore sandpipers and herons scour the shallows. Muskrats, minks, and other mammals scurry along the shore. A lake is a very busy place.

Throughout the world, lakes are in trouble because of human activity. Acid rain, chemicals from factories, fertilizer from farms, and pesticides are polluting lake waters. Fertilizers cause algae to grow uncontrollably, killing other plant life. Bacteria that decompose the dead plants use up the water's oxygen, causing fish to die. Other pollutants, like chemicals and pesticides, are linked to increased diseases, like cancer, in fish. Common loons lay their eggs at a lake's edge. Their young eat fish, which the parents find and bring to them. Acid rain in Canadian lakes has caused many fish to die, and so loons are sometimes unable to find enough food for their young. Without enough food, the chicks die. So far, the loon is not endangered, but it is being watched carefully.

We use water in many ways: we drink it, clean with it, and irrigate our farms, but we are facing a worldwide shortage of fresh water. Pollution is only part of the problem. Another is that people grow crops in places, like deserts, without adequate sources of water. Water has to be transported from lakes, rivers, and underground wells to water these dry fields.

These are all big problems. We may seem to have an endless supply of fresh water, but if we do not take care of it, it could disappear.

Dragonflies lay their eggs in water. Immature dragonflies —called nymphs— are totally aquatic. It is not known if they are at risk, but their continued survival depends on clean, healthy bodies of water.

Loons are marvelous swimmers and divers. Some of their bones are solid, which helps them dive deep. This also makes it hard for them to take off into flight.

FACTS

* *

✳ The world's largest lake, the Caspian Sea, has salt water, and was called an ocean in ancient times.

✳ All lakes are temporary. Over long periods of time they gradually disappear as they fill with sediment.

✳ The Great Salt Lake in Utah, U.S., is a habitat for many birds, but only brine shrimp can live in its very salty water.

Rivers

Rivers and their banks teem with life. Some creatures, like fish and crustaceans, spend their whole lives in the water, while others use the water as a temporary home. Beavers build dams, creating a pond as protection from predators. Wading birds catch fish and frogs along the banks. Salmon swim from their saltwater habitats into freshwater rivers to spawn.

Rivers are important to people too. They flow through our cities and towns, provide us with drinking water, irrigate our farms, and are places to play. Because they are so close to us, we often change them to suit our lives better. We build dams to control the flow of water through populated areas, change the course of their flow for our convenience, and put factories on their banks that empty chemicals into the water.

All of these changes affect nearby wildlife. The Three Gorges Dam on the Yangtze River in China was built to provide hydroelectric power. Thousands of acres of forest were cut down, cities and towns were destroyed, thousands of people had to be moved to new homes, and many species have been affected. Siberian cranes, critically endangered birds, have lost their wintering grounds because of the dam. The baiji, a species of river dolphin sometimes known as the "Goddess of the Yangtze," is now considered extinct because of changes to its river habitat.

There are many groups working to preserve rivers as natural habitats throughout the world. It is hard work, but some progress has been made. The Chinese government has begun replacing some of the forest that was cut down to build the Three Gorges Dam. Elsewhere many governments have set up conservation groups that recommend the best ways to use our rivers' resources with the least impact on their wildlife.

This spawning salmon has been caught by a bald eagle, but eagles are the least of its problems. Pollution, overfishing, loss of freshwater habitats, damming of spawning rivers, and diseases spread from salmon farms have all contributed to a drastic decrease in the salmon population.

The red-crowned crane is very large, and extremely rare. It is found in Japan, China, Korea, and Manchuria. The governments of China and Russia are beginning to protect these beautiful birds along the Amur River, one of their breeding grounds, but they are still severely endangered.

FACTS

* The Nile, which stretches for 4,135 miles (6,655 km), is the longest river in the world while the Amazon, at just under 4,000 miles (6,440 km) long, is second.

* *The Guiness Book of World Records* lists the Roe River in Montana, U.S., as the shortest river, but people in Oregon believe it is their D River. Both rivers shrink and grow according to tides, but both claim 58 feet (18 m) as the shortest length and around 200 feet (60 m) as the longest.

* The D River was named in a nationwide contest in 1940. Judges liked the short name for the shortest river.

* Baiji are one of four species of freshwater dolphins. They are nearly blind.

* There are fossils of baiji from about 25 million years ago.

FACTS

. . . .

* Coastlines are very diverse
  habitats. They can include ocean,
  marsh, coastal forest, grassland,
  sand dunes, and rivers.

* The African Penguin (a coastal
  bird), the only penguin found in
  Africa, is threatened by oil spills
  and the overfishing of its food.

Shorelines

Shorelines form the boundary between sea and land. They can be sandy or rocky; they can have grasses, shrubs, trees, or no vegetation at all. All sorts of wildlife are found along shorelines, where there is plenty to eat. All types of fish and other sea creatures feed near shorelines. Nine-tenths of all ocean species live near the coasts, giving this habitat a density of life and activity unlike any other place on earth.

The dangers to shoreline habitats are many. Oil spills and other pollutants kill water birds and animals near shore, like red-throated loons, harlequin ducks, western grebes, sea otters, and many others. Development along the shore destroys valuable habitat. Rising sea temperatures due to global warming kill many of the tiny organisms that are low on the food chain. Scientists are watching the situation very closely to see which species will be most seriously affected.

The mangrove forest is a very special shoreline habitat found in tropical areas around the world. A combination of rainforest and wetland, mangrove forests grow in the brackish water between fresh and salt water. The long bending roots of mangrove trees grab the ground to capture sediment flowing from rivers to the sea. They filter pollution, providing clean water to the ocean. Underwater, the roots provide shelter for countless species of fish and shellfish.

Mangrove forests are one of the most endangered habitats in the world. Tree roots are clogged by oil spills, and over time pollution kills the trees. People cut down whole forests for the wood, which makes good charcoal, or they fill them in for development and insect control. It is very important for the future health of the oceans that mangrove forests be preserved.

River otters were once nearly extinct because they were hunted for their fur. The River otters were also threatened because of loss of their habitats. Conservation measures have greatly improved the situation, but those that live along ocean coastlines are vulnerable to oil spills.

These roseate spoonbills nest in the mangrove trees and fish near their roots, sweeping their odd-looking bills back and forth through the water to scoop up small fish and crustaceans.

Oceans

Oceans cover about 70 percent of the earth's surface. These huge bodies of salt water are home to some of the most beautiful and mysterious plants and animals in the world. The complexity of ocean life continues to be explored by scientists, and new species are discovered every year. But even as new species are found, many others are in danger of being lost forever.

Think of the world's oceans as being one global ocean with a variety of habitats. Pelagic birds, like the albatross, spend most of their lives over deep open water, coming to shore only to nest. Some animals, like sea otters, live near the coastline where their food is abundant. Polar bears spend the Arctic summer on ice floes, hunting for seals. Arctic terns live in perpetual summer, flying from pole to pole with the seasons. Tiny plants called phytoplankton are everywhere, absorbing millions of tons of carbon dioxide each day and producing oxygen.

A lifelong love of water is one of the reasons my family and I decided to live on an island off the coast of British Columbia. One of my pleasures here is canoeing out in the bay. Paddling along the shoreline, I enjoy seeing all sorts of wildlife, like harbor seals, sea lions, and otters. Fish break the surface of the water, and birds perch on nearby rocks or fly overhead searching for a meal.

Driftnets have long been used to catch large numbers of fish, like tuna, for commercial use. Unfortunately, they also catch dolphins, whales, pelagic birds like this lysan Albatross, and sharks. Unable to escape, these creatures die and are discarded by the fishermen.

The wandering albatross takes in a lot of salt water with its food, and it has a special gland above its nose that helps filter out salt from its body.

The ocean is so vast it might seem we could not possibly destroy it, but we are. Many ocean habitats are fragile, and some effects are already being seen.

Coral reefs are the rainforests of the ocean, home to about 25% of ocean life. Coral are actually tiny animals, and the reefs have been formed over thousands of years. Coral feed on algae, which give them their beautiful colors.

The reefs are threatened in many ways. Able to exist only in a certain range of water temperatures, many—like the Great Barrier Reef near Australia—are dying as global warming increases the ocean's temperature. Other threats are pollution, overfishing, development, and damage done by boaters and divers—some of whom break off pieces of coral for souvenirs.

As with any habitat, the threats to one species affect others as well.

Orcas are large, impressive sea-going mammals that are found in oceans throughout the world. Orcas are threatened by oil spills and other pollution, habitat disturbance, overfishing of their prey fish, and intentional shooting by fishermen who see the orcas as competition.

When certain fish species die out, the birds that feed on them do not get enough to eat. Ocean scientists are just beginning to understand the complex life of coral reefs. They worry that if too much damage is done, they will not yet have the knowledge to help restore these valuable habitats.

Kelp forests are another important ocean habitat. Bull kelp is an underwater plant that grows up to 60 feet (18 meters) from the ocean floor. Many species of fish find refuge from predators like the orca among the dense growth of the kelp and lay their eggs among its fronds. Human activities like fishing and dredging destroy the kelp forests, leaving its inhabitants vulnerable. We have too often seen the damage that oil spills can do to water birds and animals, but the oil is also toxic to the kelp, and a bad spill can easily wipe out a kelp forest.

FACTS

* The Pacific Ocean is the earth's largest ocean; the Arctic Ocean is the earth's smallest.

* The longest mountain range in the world is at least 25,000 miles (40,000 km) long—and it's all under the ocean!

* The amount of garbage dumped into the ocean each year is three times more than the fish taken out.

* Most of the sun's energy that reaches the earth is stored in its oceans.

Polar Oceans

The coldest oceans in the world are located at the North and South Poles. Vast ice sheets cover much of these oceans. Pack ice forms at the edges in winter, doubling the size of the ice. Despite this forbidding climate, the ice is home and habitat to a number of hardy creatures.

The Arctic is the smallest and shallowest of earth's oceans. Warmer than Antarctica, it is populated by a great variety of wildlife. All of its inhabitants are adapted to the icy climate, either having strategies to survive the winter or migrating to warmer waters. Several land-going mammal species make their homes in the Arctic, unlike Antarctica.

In Antarctica, there is an abundance of life under the ice. Its fish and other sea creatures are admirably suited to the cold, dark conditions. Water temperatures do not change a great deal, so the sea life does not need to make seasonal adjustments. Several varieties of marine mammals—seals and whales—live there at least part of the year. And of course, penguins live on the ice and in the water, feeding on fish and krill.

Global warming is melting the Arctic ice faster than expected, which is alarming for its wildlife. Polar bears use ice floes for hunting, lying in wait to surprise seals swimming below. They take their catch onto the floe to eat. As these ice floes melt, polar bears will not be able to hunt. They may starve, and some will retreat to land for food—including human garbage—becoming vulnerable to hunting. So far, Antarctica is not affected as much, but even there ice shelves are collapsing and animals are losing their habitats.

I call this painting *"Global Warning."* The polar bear swimming in open water, with no ice in sight, reminds us of the future facing that magnificent animal with global warming.

FACTS

* The recent Census of Marine Life found 235 species of aquatic life that live in both polar oceans, many more than were known before. They include humpback whales and Blue whales, but also crustaceans, tiny creatures like worms, and snail-like pteropods.

* *Chionodraco hamatus*, an "ice fish" found in Antarctica, thrives in temperatures cold enough to freeze the blood of all other fish.

* Scientists are already noticing that many cold-loving creatures are moving further north as ocean temperatures increase.

* Cold Antarctic waters are incubators for the eggs of some species that live in warmer waters.

Epilogue

Our natural habitats are like the interlocking pieces of a jigsaw puzzle, working together to make a picture. Each piece adds something important to the puzzle. For millions of years, the world has adapted to changing conditions in the environment. Some species have disappeared and others have taken their place, but evolution has been a natural, gradual process. Now we are asking the world to change too much and too fast, and it cannot keep up.

Many people are working to try to save the world's natural habitats and their wildlife. Scientists are encouraging governments to make laws that will help slow global warming. Governments are establishing national parks and nature preserves where wildlife can roam safely. There are thousands of books, magazines, and websites dedicated to showing us what is being done to help, and what still needs to be done.

When I was a child, I belonged to a junior naturalist club. What a great place to meet people who loved nature! We took walks in local ravines as well as in the countryside where we learned just how rich our natural environment was. Experts and experienced amateurs taught us about what we saw and encouraged us to find out more. There is probably a similar group where you live.

Whether you join a group or not, get outside and explore the natural world. What can you see? Are there birds and animals? How many species can you count? What makes one species different from another? What do they eat? Where do they nest and who takes care of the young? Where do they spend the winter? Are there tadpoles and crayfish in the pond? What kind of trees and wildflowers can you name? How does the world you are exploring change from season to season?

Remember that there are children all over the world who are learning about *their* natural world and who also want to keep it safe for future children. If everyone does that, together we can make a big difference.

Glossary

Algae: Organisms that, like plants, produce oxygen by the process of photosynthesis. All seaweeds, like kelp, are algae, and there are many smaller, simpler forms as well. Algae are not classified as plants because they do not have roots, stems, or leaves, and do not get their nutrients from soil.

Amphibian: A type of animal that is fish-like when born but changes to an air-breathing animal when grown. Toads, frogs, and salamanders are amphibians.

Carnivorous: Meat-eating.

Crustacean: An animal, like lobster, crab, and shrimp, that has its skeleton on the outside in the form of a shell.

Dormant: Plant growth stops because the temperature is too cold or there is not enough moisture in the soil.

Epiphyte: A type of plant that does not grow with its roots in soil. Instead, the roots draw moisture and nutrients from the surrounding air.

Ice Shelf: A huge, thick expanse of floating ice that has formed on land and spread slowly to the ocean. It is made up entirely of fresh water (unlike pack ice, which has some salt). Ice shelves are found only in Antarctica, Greenland, and Canada.

Irrigate: Artificially watering farm fields by diverting water in from nearby rivers or lakes.

Larva: The young form of certain animals that change form completely as adults. A caterpillar is the larva of a butterfly. A tadpole is the larva of a frog or toad.

Pack Ice: A large area of floating ice that forms on the water's surface and is not attached to land. Smaller chunks of floating ice are called floes. The largest ice packs are found in the Arctic and Antarctica

Pelagic: Of the open ocean. Refers especially to birds and fish that spend the majority of their lives at sea, far from land.

Polar: Describes the regions at and near the North and South Poles. The climate is quite cold in the winter, and cool in the summer.

Temperate: A climate that has a cold winter and a hot summer.

Tropical: A climate that is warm year-round. Tropical regions are found at or near the equator.

Sediment: Small particles, especially of dirt or other matter, that is carried by streams and rivers and deposited at the river's mouth or along the shore.

Nancy Kovacs is a writer, editor, and amateur naturalist. She has done editorial work for Ontario Nature (Federation of Ontario Naturalists) and the Pontifical Institute of Mediaeval Studies Press and most recently was editor of Robert Bateman's *Backyard Birds* and *Polar Worlds*.

Vanishing Habitats was produced by Madison Press Books 1000 Yonge St., Suite 303 Toronto, Ontario M4W 2K2

Editors: Hannah Draper Diane Young

Production Coordinator: Mollie Wilkins

Art Director: Diana Sullada

Publisher: Oliver Salzmann